Is This My Home Now?
Featuring Addy

Presented by
Rescue Pups and Such
Book series inspired by real-life rescue animals.

Written and Illustrated by Connie Warsh-Wenzel
Edited by Cortney Warsh

Addy, a cute little Chihuahua, lived alone on the streets of a small town.

One day, Addy grew tired from walking around the small town.

Addy saw some lush green grass behind an old church and thought, "This looks like a good resting place."

Addy made a bed in the lush grass and lay down to rest. Satisfied with her new bed, she drifted off to sleep.

Addy dreamed of happy days when she played with her brothers and sisters and cuddled with her mother.

In the morning Addy woke up very hungry, so she left her new grassy home to find some breakfast.

A half-eaten sandwich was lying on the ground. Addy gobbled it up and loved every last bite!

After eating the sandwich, Addy was very thirsty.

She walked to a nearby park and drank some water from a refreshing pond.

Out of the blue,
Addy was caught by a long leash.

Addy was put in a truck and driven away from the park and her new grassy home.

The truck stopped at the City Animal Shelter.

There she saw many other pups locked up in kennels. Addy was so scared! Why was she taken to such a place?

A man took Addy out of the truck.
He gave her a big hug and a kiss and softly said,
"Everything's okay," as he put her into a kennel.

Addy turned to the pup in the kennel next to hers.
With tears in her eyes she asked,
"Is this my home now?" The pup replied,
"It might be. I see pups come and go but I'm still here."

The man brought Addy bowls of food and water, but she was too tired to eat or drink.

Addy curled up in her new bed and fell fast asleep.

The next day, Addy was told a lady from a rescue shelter was there to pick her up.

Addy didn't know what a "rescue shelter" was, but it sounded like something good!

The lady from the rescue shelter took Addy out of the kennel. She softly said, "Everything's okay," and gave Addy a big hug and a kiss.

Addy kissed her back and the lady giggled.

The lady drove Addy to a barn where there were many other pups.

The pups were all so excited to meet Addy! They sniffed each other to say hello and started to play.

That night, Addy turned to the pup next to her and asked, "Is this my home now?"

The pup replied, "I'm not sure. Pups come and go but I'm still here."

In the following weeks, Addy ate, played, and slept her days away. Other pups came and went, but Addy stayed at the barn.

"This must be my home now," Addy thought.

One day Addy saw a new lady at the barn.

The lady picked Addy up and softly said, "Everything's okay," then took her to the yard to play.

After they had lots of fun playing, the nice lady told Addy, "I'm going to adopt you and be your new mom." Addy didn't know what "adopt" or "new mom" meant, but they sounded like something good!

Addy's new mom took Addy to her new home.

In the house, Addy's new mom introduced her to Shane, Chase, and Lilly... her new brothers and sister!

All of the pups were so excited to meet Addy. They sniffed each other to say hello and started to play.

Addy jumped onto her new mom's lap and cuddled into a blanket.

Addy's new mom looked down at her and smiled.

Addy felt loved and safe for the first time in her life.

That night, Addy turned to Shane and said, "Please tell me this is my home now."

Shane replied, "Yes, Addy, this is your home."

"I am home. I'll never be alone or hungry again," Addy thought to herself.

Addy curled up in her new bed and smiled as she fell fast asleep.

www.ingramcontent.com/pod-product-compliance
Lightning Source LLC
Chambersburg PA
CBHW042146290426
44110CB00002B/131